SIDNEY A. D/

THE SADDLER

SHIRE PUBLICATIONS LTD

ACKNOWLEDGEMENTS

The cover photograph, by Graham Wilson Photography, shows the author at work making the panel of a saddle.

Photographs are acknowledged as follows: *Hereford Times*, pages 4 and 41; Hereford Museum, pages 11 and 17; Basil Butcher, page 14 (bottom); Donovan C. Wilson, pages 56, 58 and 61. All photographs except those on pages 4, 56, 58 and 61 are by Graham Wilson Photography.

Set in 12 point Times and printed in Great Britain by C. I. Thomas & Sons (Haverfordwest) Ltd, Press Buildings, Merlins Bridge, Haverfordwest.

Contents

The author making thread, as described in chapter 4. Here he is rubbing wax along the thread, having rolled the cords of hemp to the correct tension on the leather thread apron strapped around his waist.

1
Early memories

I was born on 2nd March 1908 on the Homend Estate, the home of Sir Edward Hopton, at Stretton Grandison, Herefordshire. My father had been a cavalryman in the Fifth Dragoon Guards and was then the coachman to Sir Edward. He was very well versed in horsemanship and had been in the Dragoon Guards at the time of Queen Victoria's Jubilee, when he was one of the guardsmen lining the streets on horseback. Sir Edward had been Governor General in Jersey and Gibraltar, and my father had travelled with him to both these places.

At the time I was born, although the Hopton family had one car and a chauffeur, they still had horses and carriages, as well as hunters, a dog-cart and a general-purpose cart for taking luggage to and from the railway station. In those days people often travelled by train and were met at the station by a horse-drawn vehicle. In our case the station was three miles away from the Homend Estate.

As a small boy, I saw how the horses were kept and looked after, for I often went to Homend with my father. My grandfather, a retired coachman, lived with us then, so there was all sorts of horse talk at home and I was brought up in a horsy world.

When the transition occurred from the horse-drawn carriage to the motorcar, the coachman in many cases became the chauffeur. The Hopton family thought my father would do likewise, and he was sent on a course of training for driving at the firm of Friars, of Aubrey Street, Hereford. This was not a great success, for my father, who was recognised as a highly skilled horseman, was not mechanically minded. His heart was never with the car, and he happily went back to the horses. I think my father had an ally in Sir Edward, who was also fond of horses. A further consideration which I think played a part was that when visitors came to the house, driving or on horseback, the horses would be handed over to the coachman to be kept warm. When the visitors were ready to depart the coachman would take the horses to the front of the house, and the departing guests usually gave a tip for this service.

Sir Edward Hopton died in 1912, when I was four years of age, and at the start of the 1914-18 war Lady Hopton left Homend and went to live at Hagley. My father's services were no longer required, so in 1914 we came to live in Hereford. The city was then a small market town with a population of about twenty-two thousand. My father took up other employment and he never went back to work with horses again.

I went to an ordinary elementary school, leaving at the age of fourteen and starting work as a saddler's apprentice from 8th May 1922. I went to work in a small saddler's shop in Broad Street, Hereford, for Mr D. L. Ellis, who employed two men.

In Hereford then the horse population far outnumbered motor cars and vans and it was considered that horses would always be used for draught work.

In the 1914-18 war the horse had been used extensively for transport and for the artillery. I can remember seeing cavalry troops being trained on the outskirts of the city. My employer was an ex-army saddler and I later met other saddlers who had served as tradesmen in the forces.

The mention of cavalry brings to mind a childish prank which could have had serious results. For a dare I threw my cap in front of a team of horses; this caused them to shy and bolt, and they galloped straight through the centre of a troop of cavalry.

Horses were used by tradesmen of all kinds. The City Council, the Great Western Railway goods and parcels department, the butcher, the baker, the grocer, the milkman and the undertaker all used horses, and many of their vehicles were of the special patterns which their particular trades had adopted, such as the baker's bread van, the milkman's float and the undertaker's hearse. Examples of these vehicles may be seen in carriage museums around the country.

A furniture van in many cases would be drawn by one horse. The words in the music hall song 'My old man said follow the van'

Homend, Stretton Grandison, the home of Sir Edward Hopton, where the author's father was coachman. The author was born on the estate.

The author's father photographed about 1890 when serving in the Fifth Dragoon Guards. Note his perfect riding position.

referred to a furniture van, and when in about 1916 we changed houses in Hereford the horse-drawn furniture van came early in the morning, was loaded up and my parents, my sister and I walked behind the van to our new home.

At the cab ranks in Broad Street and High Town, Hereford, there were cabbies' shelters, where, in winter time particularly, the cab drivers gathered and waited for their fares. The poor horses were left to stand out in the rain, with only a rug over them, until they were ready to move off. In later years I often went out to do small repairs to what was then known as the 'dash' of the cabby's vehicle where it was standing in the street.

Two doctors in Hereford also used horses and one continued doing so until about 1975. He died within a few months of retiring, aged over ninety years.

Tractors had been used during the 1914-18 war, particularly the old Fordson type, with the oval-shaped tank on top, but many farmers kept teams of horses, sometimes as many as twenty-two, and also had a pony and trap or similar vehicle to go to market.

Although the Midland Red bus service had started in Hereford in 1920, we still had the village carriers going around the villages. Sometimes they brought people into market and often they delivered groceries from Hereford. They usually had a particular hostelry at which they put up for the day so that people knew exactly where to come to them for business.

To cope with the horse population, there were in the town seven saddlers' shops that I can remember. Two of these were one-man businesses. The others had from two to five saddlers working in them. Some of these did a lot of work in the market, dealing with a large amount of second-hand war equipment. After the 1914-18 war horses were not much used for military purposes and a vast amount of equipment made for the army became available, some of which was adapted for ordinary work.

There were three carriage builders in Hereford, and I remember watching their skilled craftsmen at work. There were several trades involved in carriage building, including the carriage smith or coach smith, the carriage painter, the carriage upholsterer, and the budget trimmer, who did all the patent leather work on the sides of the carriage.

There were seven blacksmiths' shops in Hereford, to cope with the shoeing, three or four corn or forage merchants and three veterinary surgeons, for whom the care of the horse was a large part of their work.

There were two horsebreakers, one of whom had his yard at the end of the street in which I lived, so I saw him in operation for many years. He used a gig, which was a vehicle with very long shafts, so that the horse in training did not do any damage if it kicked out. On the vehicle was a platform for a groom to ride on, so that he could leap quickly down from his position and run to the horse's head to calm and control him.

Another tackle used in breaking horses was the 'dumb jockey', which consisted of cross pieces of wood fitted on a padded roller, enabling reins to be fitted from the bit to the normal position held by the rider. In breaking work the side reins are often fitted with rubber springs to take the jar out of any quick movement of the horse's head.

The breaking outfit in most common use is a roller with a wide

The saddler's shop in Broad Street, Hereford, where the author was apprenticed in 1922. Mr D. L. Ellis, his employer, is the man on the left.

range of adjustments for size, fitted with dees and rings to take side reins and long reins. To prevent the roller moving forward a crupper is fitted. This is a strap arrangement which fits along the horse's back and ends with the dock, which goes under the animal's tail. Most docks are stuffed with linseed and stretched to shape. In this case these would also be made to buckle in place on the crupper for ease in fitting on an untrained animal.

With this roller goes a head harness known as a breaking cavesson. This has a padded noseband on which is mounted a nose iron with rings to take a lunging rein, and provision is made for a bit to be buckled in place, usually a plain Barmouth.

For training a racehorse there are pieces of equipment used which the general saddler is seldom called upon to make. Horses were bred on a number of farms and we sometimes supplied a horsehair rope used in the initial training of a foal, because it had a 'spring' effect.

A number of public houses had stabling so that when people came into market they could leave their horses and carts there while they did their business. It was important to keep the horses warm when they came in sweating from their journey into the city.

The Royal George in Widemarsh Street, Hereford, had stabling at the rear, but no room for the carts, so that these were left in the street. The shafts of the carts were placed on the ground, and the wheels of the next cart were run over the top of them, so forming a tight queue of carts and thus conserving space. On Market Fair days I have often seen lines of vehicles some hundred yards long, from the Royal George right down to Blackfriars Street.

Usually these public houses had an ostler, or hostler, and a market room. An ostler's box can still be seen in the village of Shoreham, Kent. People would send their groceries to the Royal George, for example, stating that they were leaving at, say, four o'clock that afternoon. These would go in the market room, usually a small room with rows of shelves around it upon which the goods were put. Occasionally parcels would be ordered, and these too would be sent out with the local carrier.

There are four main breeds of carthorse – the Shire, the Percheron, the Clydesdale and the Suffolk – but in Herefordshire the Shire held pride of place.

Hereford City Council carried out all its work with the help of horses. In Stonebow Road the council had stables, where about twenty carthorses were kept. They were used for carting stone, collecting rubbish, sweeping and watering the streets. Watering the streets in summertime was an essential service in the days before the tarmacadam road.

I also remember the horse-drawn snowplough, which was con-

High Town, Hereford, during the horse age.

structed out of two large V-shaped pieces of wood and drawn by two horses.

The Hereford saddlers each in turn had the work of repairing the harness of the council's Shire horses. Our shop would have the work for six months and then the work went to the next saddler in turn. Just before I started, Mr Ellis's shop had received an order for about a dozen sets of new harness.

The Great Western Railway delivered heavy goods from the railway station on large flat drays drawn by big carthorses. The railway had special bays at the station where the wagons were unloaded.

The horses used for passenger parcels were usually smaller and lighter, coming somewhere between a large carriage horse and a carthorse in size. They drew covered vans for this work and were called 'heavy vanners'.

The chandler used a similar horse, drawing a van usually with a cover of black canvas with the owner's name painted on it. He sold soap, soap powders, buckets, spades and other items and usually carried a tank of paraffin aboard too. His trade was based on household requirements and rounds were made to various villages on certain days. The chandler took orders from householders for items he did not have with him and brought them back the following week.

One chandler I knew of used to carry a bugle, and when the houses were some way from the road he would draw up his horse and give a toot on the bugle to warn the inhabitants he was there. If they did not require anything he would be waved on his way.

The breweries used very big drays drawn by pairs of carthorses, but there were not many of these 'pair horse drays' in use in the city. They were a marvellous sight when they were in good condition, and they could pull some very heavy loads. Hauliers and builders also used carthorses, as did timber hauliers. Their vehicles were flat, four-wheeled and long enough to carry building materials, lengths of wood, ladders and other large items. Sometimes the wood and other materials would extend from the cart well over the horses' backs. Short two-wheeled tip carts were also used extensively by builders, hauliers and on the land.

In this day of powerful bulldozers and mechanical diggers it is hard to recall that in an earlier age all the earth on the road was moved by pick and shovel, with wheelbarrows. Earth was carted away by horse and cart, mostly by means of tip carts. Enormous work was done by men and horses in the building of canals, roads and railways. Horses carried the bricks, slates and wood for all construction works.

Timber haulage was the hardest type of work the horse was called upon to perform, apart from wartime work. The hauliers' businesses were usually very small and they operated on a piecework basis.

First of all, to move the felled timber from the wood, strong chains were placed around the trunk and it was then dragged along the ground. This was called 'tushing' it. At the edge of the wood the timber was loaded on to a long timber carriage.

The timber wagon teams often consisted of five or even six horses. They carted the timber to the nearest station or direct to the local sawmill, and this was done on a tonnage basis. The work was virtually slavery for the horses and men.

There was very little money to spend on the horses and many timber hauliers used animals that had seen their best days. Those poor beasts were worked very hard indeed. When the timber teamster cracked the whip the horses went very nearly to the ground on their bellies in order to move the wood, and they had to put every ounce they had into pulling the wagon. They knew what the whip meant to them. I was very glad to see the big diesel timber carriages taking over from the horse.

There were still quite a number of private horses, cobs and ponies. Horses were the largest, starting at a height of about sixteen hands. Cobs were about fourteen hands, the Welsh Cob being one of the best known breeds. Ponies were smaller still but they could do their own particular job. A milkman would use a pony to pull a cart that was not carrying any great weight, such as a few churns of milk. Very often ponies were quick-trotting too.

Big gig horses were used for drawing carriages. I cannot remember many pair-horse outfits, but I do remember one which belonged to a lady on Aylestone Hill, Hereford, the horses always being kept in tip-top condition.

Then there were the horse-drawn fire engines. I recall seeing the 'Steamer' turn out once, drawn by two horses, with one fireman stoking the fire and the steam coming out as it raced by.

I believe, however, that outside Hereford, certainly in the larger cities, the horse population was declining much more quickly.

A smartly turned-out carriage and pair. The harness bears the insignia of its aristocratic owner.

ABOVE: *Shaft horse or thiller in cart harness or short gears. Note the cart saddle and back chain to carry the weight of the shafts, and also the breeching for the horse to hold back the load.*
BELOW: *A timber wagon hauled by a team of six horses.*

2
The saddlery trade

The saddlery trade is divided into several branches. I started in a general saddler's business, a type of which there were hundreds up and down the country. In the main we were harnessmakers, and a lot of our work was making and mending black harness. Of course, there was some saddle work, but it was mainly for the farmer who wanted a horse to ride round his stock or for general purposes. We were often called upon to make special cases to carry and protect various musical and scientific instruments, lecture cases and briefcases of particular design. We also repaired all kinds of travel goods, trunks, suitcases, hatboxes and many other items.

Most saddlers bought their riding saddles and their bridlework from the wholesale makers, mainly from Walsall. Even today the nickname for the Walsall football team is the 'Saddlers'.

In the wholesale business there were many divisions. There were saddlemakers, riding saddlemakers, brown saddlers and black saddlers – these were the people who made gig saddles (the small pads seen on the harness which carried the weight of the shafts). There were bridle cutters, harnessmakers, collarmakers and a host of specialist firms who made dog collars, muzzles, leads, bags, braces, purses, wallets, military equipment and much more besides. Nearly all of this was piecework and in most instances it was very low-priced as well.

In most towns there were, however, one or two shops which specialised in the making of 'new work', for example new sets of harness. Some firms were specialists in the making of cart harness, and others in the making and repairing of driving harness. In London in particular there were specialist saddlers, who made riding saddles and made and cut bridles, their work being all brown. They were classified as brown saddlers accordingly.

Most of the local gentry had their London saddlers, where they bought their special saddles and sent them for repair. They went there to be measured, having their saddles made to measure. Some of them did give us support in the country by bringing us a certain amount of repair work and buying some of the accessories which they used.

There were also many subsidiary trades, such as the bucklemakers, chainmakers, bitmakers, brush and comb manufacturers.

The bitmakers were very important, for until the First World War most riding bits and stirrup irons were made of hand-forged steel. It was not thought to be safe to use other metals. However, they have since been replaced by nickel bits and stirrups and also by stainless steel which is easier to keep clean. In the old days the steel bits required a tremendous amount of care and after use they had to be taken off, cleaned, washed, dried and burnished with a chain burnisher.

All the pieces which could be taken off the bridle were hand-forged steel and were kept in a glass-fronted and baize-lined case over the fireplace of the stable room.

The bits on carriage harness could also be removed by unbuckling the 'billet' straps on the bridle. On most riding bridles the bits were sewn directly on to the reins and cheeks. The modern practice is to use hook-stud fastenings and occasionally buckle billets for, whereas in stables of years gone by there were often a number of bridles with different types of bit, today many riders have only one bridle and want to be able to change bits.

The saddler even used to make parts for early motorcars. There were various strappings for securing the spare tyre and for holding down the goods, and some of the older cars had leather clutches, for which we fitted new clutch leathers. On the higher grades of motorcar, such as Wolseleys and Daimlers, the springs and underneath parts were covered with leather gaiters and many of the movements of the steering lock were also covered with leather protectors.

The first few months of the saddler's year were quiet, but about March when the land was being got into shape for the spring harvest, and later for the hay harvest, there would be emergency jobs for us. After that we used to have rush jobs where there had been temporary repairs made with nails or wire. Farmers wanted the tackle ready immediately for use in time for the corn harvest.

This was a very busy time of year since cart collars and saddles were brought in to us to be relined and repadded. The collar was built on a straw base, one side being covered with serge and the other side with leather. The cart saddle panels were basically straw with a flock covering under the collar check or serge.

At harvest time we used to be busy repairing the binder-canvases, which usually needed new straps. The combine harvester has no canvases, but is fitted with augers which handle the corn. Usually it was a case of 'We want this tomorrow – we're in the middle of cutting'.

In winter time, when work slackened off again, and between the two harvests we went to work in the country, taking all our tools and equipment to the farms to repair the harness on the premises.

The usual routine was for one or two men to go and stay for a night

A hedger. Making the special gloves or mitts for hedgers was a valuable part of the author's work, and he also made yorks – the leather straps worn by many farmworkers tied round the legs just below the knee.

or two. In later years we had a bigger staff and arranged for three saddlers to go for one day, starting at six in the morning and working to nine at night. If they did not finish the work that day they would bring what remained back with them to complete in the shop.

At the farm, the farmer used to take a door off the barn or stables and place it over a couple of oil drums to make a workbench. A couple of chairs from the house would be brought for us to sit on. The farmer would more often than not supply the straw for the saddle and collar linings and he often wanted to supply the wool as well. We used to be quite happy to use parts of a fleece, but we drew the line at 'tailings' (little bits of wool) since it took so much time to use them.

Very often the farm carter would bring the work to us. After it was done he would scrub it in a pail of water, and his mate would slap some black oil on it. The wood of the hames was then covered with red paint, which was like treacle in its consistency.

The farmer would ask for allowances to be made for the number of meals he had supplied to the men, for accommodation costs if he had had to put them up overnight and for fetching the saddlers and taking them back. By the time we had made these deductions, together with the fact that we would not get another job from that particular farmer for some months, it was not a satisfactory operation for us and we soon stopped going to farms to work.

We also made and repaired driving belts for the farm, and one of the hardest jobs I ever remember doing was to sew by hand along both sides of a seventy-five foot Balata driving belt. Another job was the cutting of special washers for pumps.

To the farm labourer we sold patent leather shirt collars and 'yorks', which were straps about three quarters of an inch wide by twenty inches long. These were worn around the legs just below the knee, the trousers being pulled up slightly before fastening them. This made the trousers loose at the knee and kept the bottoms out of the mud. They would also prevent a rat from running up the trouser leg when a labourer was standing on a rick of corn when threshing.

Farm labourers of this period all wore heavy nailed boots with corduroy trousers or boots with breeches and leggings, which we sold and repaired. Many grooms wore breeches and leggings, but with lightweight boots, and their calfskin leggings were highly polished. I wore leggings when I started school at Stretton Grandison and I believe that a well made strong pair of leather boots was a much more comfortable proposition than wellington boots for walking across the fields all day.

At our shop we also sold a whole range of horse requisites, such as brushes, soaps, oils, plough reins, ointments for sores on horses' backs and shoulders, blankets and many other items.

3
My apprenticeship

My early work as an apprentice consisted of general help to all the staff. I began the day by sweeping out the shop and workshop, shaking the mat and sweeping the pavement, which consisted of stone flags. I had to clean the employer's workbench, for he worked with us, and do the general dusting of the shop. It was supposed to take an hour for me to do all that. As an apprentice I was never allowed to spend time hanging around doing nothing. I was general errand boy, post boy and bank boy, and I often went out to collect or deliver harness or trunks.

We kept sets of cart harness in stock, as 'long' and 'short' gears, long gears for the leader horse or horses and short for the shaft horse. The short gear harness was also known as 'thiller' harness. I was expected to clean the brasswork on those sets periodically.

The saddler's shop was a converted dwelling house and my employer had, prior to the 1914-18 war, worked for the previous owner. Then he had taken over the shop on his own account. He had been married a couple of years or so when I went to work for him, and he and his wife lived over the shop.

What had been the front downstairs room of the original house was then the shop, and the living room was the workshop, whilst an end wall had been removed, and a small yard at the back had been covered in with glass. A back door opened out on to the cathedral close. The heating we had was from an open coal fire, but we had no sanitation on the premises for the staff, and so we were obliged to go across to the public house and use their outside toilet. We washed our hands with soft soap, one of the trade perquisites, under the cold water taps and dried them with our work aprons.

There were no tea breaks of course, and we worked steadily through from eight a.m. to six p.m. with a dinner break from one until two. If we wanted to take lunch with us in the morning it was opened on the workbench and eaten while we worked.

Wednesday was market day, as it still is in Hereford, and was very often a day of great excitement and rush. Someone might call and say: 'I've broken my harness coming to town this morning. Repair it for me to go back. I'm going to leave it at such and such a place.' Off I would go to collect the harness, bring it back to the shop, get it repaired and then take it back to the owner to drive home.

I used to hate to go to the Black Swan in Widemarsh Street, Hereford, which had a very narrow stable for the horses. When there were a number of horses in there, all sweating and steaming, tied down each side with their backs to the centre, they were practically touching. The ostler would say to me: 'There you are boy. It's the second one from the right, up on the top deck.'

I would have to make my way, pushing and shoving through those horses, to get the harness off and take it back. When I brought it back for the man to collect, the ostler would very quickly say: 'Put it down by the harness room there, boy. I'll see to that.' It was his way of making sure that I would get no tip for taking it back.

As boys we were always on the lookout for the farmer who came along and wanted to stop a few minutes to do some business, so that we could stand holding the horse's head for half an hour for the grand sum of threepence. When I was an apprentice, occasionally a customer would come to the shop with a restive horse and I would go and stand by his head while the business was being transacted.

I often had to deal with customers outside the shop who were collecting repairs. My job would be to take the work out to them, collect the money and see them on their way. We had one old gentleman and nothing was right for him. Every time I took anything out he would say: 'Ooh, boy! It's too dear, it's too dear! Can't you take something off it?' Once, when it was a small job of about three shillings and sixpence, I said to him: 'Yes, give me three shillings and that will do.' He said: 'You go and ask Mr Ellis.' I said: 'Right, I will.' My employer said: 'You're not to take anything off. Three shillings and sixpence is the charge.' When I returned to the customer, he said: 'Oh, but you said three shillings.' I said: 'Yes, but that was before you sent me back to see Mr Ellis.'

I was wise to this man ever afterwards, and any job I took out to him I always put on sixpence and when I let him have it I would say: 'Look, I'll take off sixpence for you, but don't you let on I did it.'

At that time the bicycle was in great use, and I used it like many other boys for all sorts of things. After a couple of years practice I became adept at carrying many different items while riding a bicycle. I never quite reached the heights of one of the lads who worked with us in later years, who could put a full-sized table-tennis table on his bicycle, balanced on the pedal, and push it a mile out of town to deliver it. I was, however, able often to take a complete set of driving harness on my shoulder and ride at the same time.

If the load we wanted to fetch or carry was a bit heavier than usual we often had to use a hand truck which we borrowed from a public house across the road. Hand trucks usually had the owner's name painted on the side and, like horse-drawn vehicles, many were specialist trucks for a particular trade. The baker had a box truck with double doors at the end and places inside it for trays. The upholsterer had a long-handled truck with a very big, flat top and no sides; the wheels were tucked away underneath. A settee could be put on top of it, secured with a piece of webbing, and I often used to see an oldish gentleman trundling down the street with a load much bigger than himself.

The milkman had a small three-wheeled handcart with one milk churn, usually well-polished, and with the brasswork shining. He also had an oval-shaped can, holding two gallons, and when he lifted the lid off it a bar could be seen inside on which hung his measures, half-pint and pint, for measuring out milk at the customer's door.

A sewing machine firm had a special handcart on which to take their treadle sewing machines about, and a chandler's and iron-monger's business in Hereford had little carts consisting of baskets, three feet by eighteen inches, on three wheels. That firm always employed delivery girls fourteen years of age and straight from school.

My employer worked at the bench with me and he and I had to share all the sales part of the work. We also had a little lock-up shop

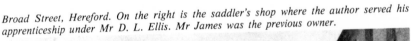

Broad Street, Hereford. On the right is the saddler's shop where the author served his apprenticeship under Mr D. L. Ellis. Mr James was the previous owner.

in Pontrilas, Herefordshire, which we opened on Friday, which was market day there.

One day there was a car parked in Palace Yard, Hereford, near the shop. The chauffeur went to reverse the car in the yard (it was a big Ruston-Hornsby) but he caught his arm on the car throttle, which was a control lever on the steering column. The car shot back and went through Madam Mountstephen's shop window, knocking a lady through the glass. At our shop there was a rather high step looking over the scene and my mate and I watched for quite a while. Eventually we went back in and later on my employer came in and said to me that there had been a crash over the way. I then replied: 'We have been pretty busy today here. Although there was a crash, we didn't have much time to see it.'

Later on that day I went for the *Hereford Times* newspaper for my employer and he opened it to look at it on the bench. He read for a while and then said to me: 'You told me you were pretty busy, but you weren't too busy to stand and have a good look at it.' There was a picture of the crash, and it showed my mate and me, in our aprons, standing there watching.

According to my indentures, I was obliged to attend night school during the five years of my apprenticeship. I took book-keeping and English with general subjects, and a section on woodworking, which proved very useful to me.

I also attended the local art school and did art leatherwork, learning to do embossed leatherwork, which I have done on many occasions since.

4
Making thread and stitching

The first thing a saddler's apprentice had to learn was to make threads and to sew, for at that time we stitched everything by hand. We used hemp and flax in different grades and numbers, for example a three-cord thread in number fifteen or four-cord of best common hemp, and so on. It was chosen to suit the work in hand, for colour and number of stitches per inch.

The saddler, in the days of high-class harnessmaking, used to sew about fourteen stitches to the inch, up to sixteen stitches to the inch in finer work. I have done many hours of stitching bridlework with silk thread at twelve stitches per inch but nowadays the finest work would be nine or ten to the inch and most only six or seven.

First of all the saddler put on a leather 'thread apron', about ten inches by six inches, which was placed well over the right thigh with a strap round the waist. He then took a ball of hemp and a ball of wax. Holding one end of the hemp in the left hand, with his right he led it round a hook attached to the bench and back to his left hand. To cut it he rolled the hemp on the apron to untwist the fibres and gently pulled it apart. Having cut the required number of cords, he rubbed a little wax on the ends, and then, rolling the ends first, he took them one at a time and rolled them on his apron to the necessary tension and then proceeded to rub the wax along the thread.

The thread produced in this way had a lovely tapered point to thread on to the blunt-pointed saddler's needles, and it enabled him to sew that much faster.

For sewing brown harness with brass furniture, we used yellow thread; with nickel furniture the thread would be white. Nearly all bridlework and certainly all riding saddles were sewn with white thread. In these cases the thread used would be made using beeswax as the binding material.

All black harness, driving or cart harness would be sewn with black wax thread. The saddler made his own black wax from best Swedish pitch, rosin and some form of grease. We had a special cast iron pot kept for this purpose. The mixture was boiled and we varied the amount of grease depending on whether it was summer or winter. More grease was added in winter. When ready we poured the boiling mixture into a bucket half-filled with cold water and worked the

Cutting a strap from brown leather, using a plough gauge.

molten wax with our hands. As this began to cool we were able to lift it out of the bucket for short periods to carry out a pulling process.

The cold water formed a very thin skin on the wax, and it was important to keep this and our hands wet to prevent adhesion or burning. It was made into a long sausage and cut into lengths, which we stored in the bucket of water and used as needed. Other saddlers put it in flour to keep.

The secret of the old harnessmakers was to use a black wax thread, made as I have described, with a small sewing awl. The friction as the threads were drawn through the hole in the leather caused the wax to melt and fill the hole, so that even when the surface of the thread had worn off it left a row of what looked like rivets.

There are two types of sewing which cover a large part of the work, 'double-handed' and 'back-hand'.

The sewing already referred to is double-handed and for this an awl with a blade which cuts a diamond-shaped hole is used. After this the thread is passed through the hole from both sides and pulled tight, using both hands, the work being held meanwhile by means of a wooden

Levelling the thickness of a strap in a hand splitting machine.

Using an edge-shave to remove the sharp edges of a strap.

clamp, which in turn is held between the saddler's knees.

Back-hand stitching is done with a single thread and makes a short stitch on the topside and a long one on the bottom. This is very useful for stitching leather to cloth, the long stitch being on the cloth side.

For marking out the work the pricking iron is used. This is tapped lightly into the surface of the leather along the line of sewing. Sometimes a wheel pricker would be used, but this tool was never very popular with the tradesmen. The marks made were only meant to show the position and angle of each stitch.

Stitching was a very important part of the work of the saddler. If he was ever going to be a high-grade craftsman a saddler must first of all be a first-class stitcher. In some cases people learned to be hand stitchers only and never learned to do any other part of the business. Even then it was a three-year apprenticeship. The art of putting the awl in the leather at a proper angle took a long time to acquire. One had to be able to put the top stitch in the groove and pick up the groove on the bottom side accurately each time and the tensions of the stitches had to be correct.

In the pre-1914 days many women, in the Walsall area in par-

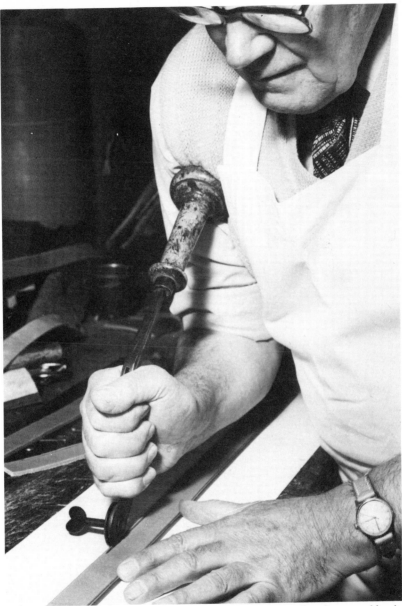

The tool called the shoulder crease is used hot to apply the vein mark and to set and harden the edges of the leather.

A prickling iron is used to mark the spaces for hand sewing, in this case seven stitches per inch. Irons range in size from four to sixteen stitches per inch.

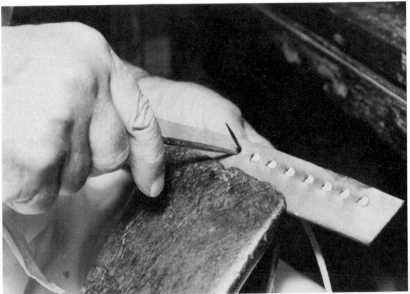

Spotting with a thong. In this type of sewing a narrow strip of horsehide is threaded backwards and forwards through diamond-shaped holes using a large-eyed needle.

ticular, took on piecework sewing in their own homes. It was quite a common sight to see the end of a harness trace coming out through the front-room window of a house.

Saddlers were so particular over the standard of stitching that any threads or stitches which were pulled in too tightly on the top side were known as 'dead men'. Saddlers had deductions made in their pay for 'dead men' found on finished jobs.

Spotting with a thong is another of the saddler's arts, not to be confused with edge thonging done by leathercraft students. The saddler takes a piece of white horsehide and with a handknife cuts a strip of leather about a quarter of an inch wide. This is pointed at one end and then damped, greased and threaded into a large-eyed needle. Diamond-shaped holes are made with a large awl and the lace is threaded backwards and forwards. The saddler works to a line and judges the spaces by eye, and it is important to keep the lace running flat. This sewing is used in cart work, for hedging gloves and for sewing the splices of heavy leather driving belts.

After learning to make threads and to sew, the apprentice also had to do the dirty jobs such as the blacking of the collar wales. These were made in brown leather, and we had first to scour them with soda

ABOVE: *The saddler's round knife is one of his most versatile tools. Here it is being used to make a splice.*
BELOW: *A strap is tacked together ready for sewing. In some cases it would be glued.*

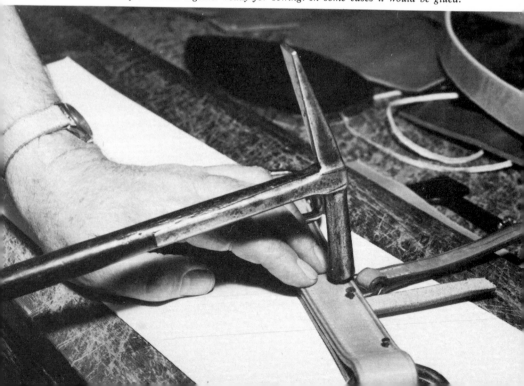

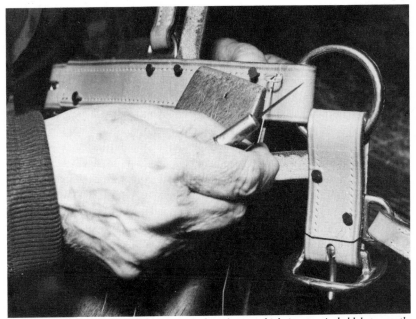

Hand sewing. The work is held in a wooden clamp, which in turn is held between the saddler's knees. This leaves both hands free to manipulate the thread. The holes for the thread are made one at a time as work progresses.

water to help break up the grease, thus allowing the dye to penetrate. There was the blacking of the edges to be done after using the edge-shaves to round the edges of the leather. Race marks were blacked in also and edges burnished. A number of harness parts were made from heavy brown leather and also required blacking.

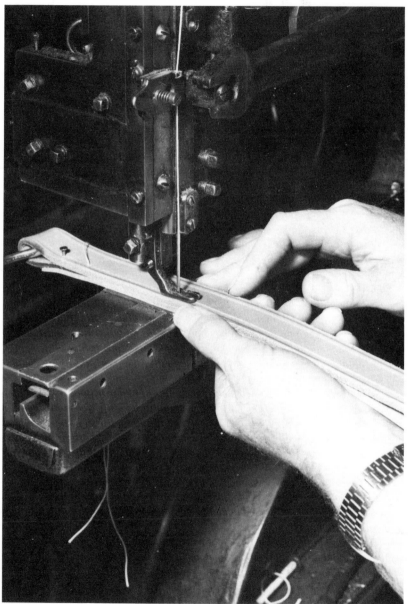

Machine sewing on harness work is only satisfactory on straight seams. All loops and such like are hand sewn.

5
Making gig harness

Most of the harness we made was black, but occasionally we had orders for brown. There were three main sizes, for the horse, cob and pony. These sizes overlap and cover animals from about twelve hands to seventeen hands.

The backbands and traces each had four rows of sewing throughout their length and that would entail several days non-stop sewing by hand. When work was short, a backband and a pair of traces were often made up but left unfinished, to wait for an order for a set of gig harness.

A pair of traces for a horse of gig size would be six feet long by one and a half inches in width; for a cob, they would be five feet six inches long by one and three eighths of an inch wide, whilst a set of pony traces would be five feet long by one and a quarter inches wide. Below the size of the pony came the small pony, and above the horse we had the van-size horse in smaller and larger sizes.

The initial part of an order for a set of harness would deal with the colour of it – black or brown – and the kind of furniture, the metal fittings, whether it was to be brass or nickel, West End pattern or Bristol pattern. West End pattern is a popular type of buckle, the sides of which are cylindrical. The Bristol pattern is a flat buckle, and much more showy. Gipsies were very fond of Bristol-type buckles, but they always wanted their work in nickel, and they liked nickel loops instead of leather loops, which made the harness showy also. I have made quite a few sets for them. They were good people with whom to deal; although they would drive a hard bargain, as soon as the goods were ready there was always instant cash to pay for it. There were many other types of buckle which had been available in times past, but it was no use starting to use these without a complete set of furniture as one could get half way and then discover that the particular pattern was not being made any more.

There were decisions to be made about the type of pad, whether or not it should have a patent leather top, and whether the winkers should be patent leather or not. A farmer might want a smart turnout just for driving into town, and he would want it with patent leather. If he only needed it for putting in a rough cart for general work he would not want anything so elaborate.

Before my time, when a set of harness was ordered for one of the gentry families, the coachman would bring in his patron's seal to make an impression in wax, from which would be made a mould of the monograms or crests of the patron. A bishop would have a mitre as part of the insignia. Special castings would be made in nickel or brass. The very highest grade of harness furniture was made from brass and was given a heavy coat of silver plate. There would only be a small number of these castings, but the bucklemaker would surely have kept his mould for further orders.

This harness work is just for gig harness. It is not pair-horse harness or for four-in-hands. We no longer made either of these or the special lightweight gig harness of earlier years, when young bloods used to drive these gigs with a fast-moving stallion, rather like the youth of today with his 'hotted-up' sports car.

For ordinary purposes the bearing rein was not used. No one wanted to see a coal-cart horse pulling a cart with a bearing rein holding his head up when he needed his head down to put his weight into the job. But for a light gig behind a fiery stallion a bearing rein was used, not least because when a horse has got his head up he cannot kick to do any real harm. In a racing sulky, still used today and popular in America, the driver sits on a little seat right behind the horse's heels, just being carried on two wheels and apparently very vulnerable if the horse were to kick. But the horse cannot kick as his head is held up by a similar arrangement to a bearing rein known as an overcheck.

The first pieces of harness to be cut out would be the backband, the traces and the breeching, as these had the longest amount of sewing. Then the other parts would be cut out and finished.

The backband is a strap which completely encircles the horse's body. The top centre part of the backband passes through a hole in the gig saddle and on each side is buckled a shaft tug, through which the shafts pass.

The bridlework on gig and cob harness would be cut three quarters of an inch wide, and the only decision to be made was the type of loops to use. The loop is a little strip of leather under which one tucks the end of the strap after buckling, as on a belt. In some types of harness we use very long loops. In a pipe-looped cheek one long loop replaced five small ones, and there was a lot of fancy work done on them called creasing. The same principle applied with hame tugs and shaft tugs and these would be 'creased' up, this being known as pipe looping.

Horse collars were a specialist's job, and in most cases the light gig and driving collars were made outright by the collarmaker. Harness collars were made from straw with a thin layer of flock under a lining

ABOVE: *The saddler uses his spokeshave to round the edges of thick work before colouring and burnishing.*
BELOW: *Close-up of a pipe loop, showing how the decoration is done, one line at a time, with a hot iron.*

of leather or blue cloth, while the outer covering was leather, patent leather, canvas or sometimes plaited rush, which was very light and used in summertime.

There were a number of qualities and styles of collar. Possibly the most common was what was known as the stage collar. It was made of leather outside, with a blue serge lining. On the front edge of the collar was a rim which was known as the pipe or wale. The hames fitted into the groove between the narrow piping and the main body of the collar, being held in place by a small strap, top and bottom. Before the hames were fitted to the collar, the hame tugs would have been made and attached with rivets, and special clips were put on known as hame clips.

If we were dealing with good-quality harness the skirts of the saddle would have a pattern matching that of the winkers. The gig saddle top was always left plain for the correct type of pedestal to be fitted but the skirts would be punched out and sockets fitted for the terrets, the rings through which the reins ran.

About the turn of the century the sockets for the terrets were standardised but before that each bucklemaker made his own dies.

The breeching and straps were straightforward to make. The breeching goes round the rear of the horse and was held up by the loin strap, which went over the loins of the horse. This was split at each end to make four points, each buckled to a tug, so that it was lifted up and held level and in place. There was a ring at each end of the breeching, and a strap going forward to loops on the shaft, so that when the horse held back he was pulling back on the shafts.

To keep the saddle stable and prevent it riding forward, another piece of harness, known as the crupper, ran along the top of the back. This ended in a loop of leather known as the dock, which went under the horse's tail. The dock was made of a piece of pliable leather, grooved top and bottom, folded over and stitched, then stuffed with linseed. We used a small tool to stuff the linseed inside and to break it up as it was put in. This released the linseed oil, which worked out into the leather and kept it supple for many years. After that the dock was shaped on a block to the proper shape before it was stitched on the crupper and left to dry.

The reins, if they were of high quality, were brown right through from the horse's mouth to the driver's hands. In cheaper sets and in later years the first part, known as the draught, from the horse's mouth halfway to the hands, would be black and the hand parts brown.

One of the last sets of good harness that I made was just before the Second World War when I made a 'lined' set, which in effect meant

Punching holes in a strap. The base is a block of lead.

the strappings were all lined, and a special dock known as a double dock was made for it.

Although it sounds very straightforward to make this harness, the finishing and burnishing of the edges took a great deal of time, as did the stitching, the fine stitching in particular.

To finish off one trace would mean first of all spoke-shaving the edges flat. The traces were created from three thicknesses of leather, two thicker pieces with a very thin piece between them. Next, one would take a number seven edge-shave and shave off the four corners and finally finished off by using the spokeshave to bevel it. It would be blacked, polished and greased. There were tricks of the trade which are hard to believe. For instance, after greasing the leather we would rub it down with brown paper to polish it. That would bring up a gloss like glass.

There were small jobs that even a junior apprentice of a month or two's training was able to do to help, such as little bits of sewing which were not too much on show. He naturally still had plenty to do with blacking and polishing.

The final task was the punching of the holes for the buckles; then it would be the apprentice's job to clean all the metalwork, and one of the workmen would give the leather a final coat of leather varnish. This was applied warm, with a piece of sponge, and it had a most pungent smell.

6
Making cart harness

In the making of cart harness, we used a tool which we never used on trap or driving harness, and that was the adjustable race compass, which cut a very shallow groove from an eighth of an inch to six inches from the edge of the leather. There was usually a double row of race marks put in the leather. These were blacked in and the stitching would go on the inside line. This sank the stitches partly into the surface of the leather, so that they would wear less and last much longer.

The body of the collar was made by the collarmaker, and we bought this ready made, but the outside finish of the leather was our job. We first of all capped it at the end of the pipe, putting a leather cap over the top to hold the top hame strap in position.

The side pieces were cut out of the belly part of the hide and soaked in water for several days. Then they were stretched around the outside of the collar and stitched with a white thong and a big six-inch needle. The other edge would be stitched right into the corner of the wale.

To keep the rim out for the hames to fit into, we hammered a rope to make grooves. Two pads were added to keep the chains or traces clear of the horse's shoulders. Sometimes we used brown leather but often it was black. When soaked the black dye and grease came to the surface and we used a bag apron over our aprons, for we were plastered in black dye when doing this work. It was a filthy job.

Repairing and relining the collars was very hard work and so was nearly all cart harness repair work. The action of sun and rain on the leather made it very hard and few farmers spent time or money on cleaning and oiling their harness.

All the sewing was done with six-inch collar needles and these were pushed through the work with a saddler's palm iron. The sewing materials were tarred twine, soft twine and horsehide laces.

The straw part of the collars was often topped up with a new layer of straw and in some cases the straw was completely replaced before the new lining and padding were put in place. Individual saddlers had their own methods of doing this work but the end result was much the same.

The cart saddle panel was made as a separate part as in other saddle work. It was cut from firm leather and the lining was sewn in; then it was stuffed with straw and padding. As with collars there were several methods and styles.

Show harness and local horse shows went out in the 1920s. I can just remember the last of the Hereford horse shows held on the Hereford football ground about 1924. However, there is now a new interest in driving and driving competitions. The Horse of the Year Show and other events which we see on television have created a much wider public interest than was possible forty or fifty years ago.

Special harness was made for carthorses for show purposes. The big heavy Percherons, Suffolks, Shires and Clydesdales were used by the breweries, and they were up to a point a form of advertisement. They are coming back into use because, for short journeys, they are a better proposition than lorries.

The type of equipment they used at big shows such as the Three Counties Show or Royal Show was of a particular kind and not for everyday use. I have seen sets in recent years where the chainwork was chromium-plated and the harness was light and showy with brasswork fitted on, but those were not working outfits. But in times past, at local shows in particular, the horses wore the harness they used every day, so that anyone could take part and still have a chance of winning.

The art of horse ploughing with a pair is still kept on, despite tractor ploughing. Even tractor shows have a horse section. For this sort of thing one could use ordinary working horses with straightforward harness. Very often the sets were also designed with lots of fancy pieces which would be screwed into place.

Carters would take their teams of horses to town with ribbons and bells, to make a striking display. The outfits belonged often to the carters themselves, and not to the farmers. They took them from one place to another. I have made many types of items of general use for the carters.

When the big Shires were taken round the road by the groom they were fitted with a fanciful roller with colours. There was a show bridle with inlets in the cheeks, of patent leather, of blues and other colours. To control the animals, in addition to the roller they would put on bearing reins from the mouth to the roller. The groom would put a side rein on the offside, fitted from the side of the roller to the horse's mouth, and from the nearside there would be a leading rein. Coupled with that rein, they often used a special fitting on the end of the rein with a bar. The rein started from the mouth with a short piece of chain which went through a ring on the nearside of the bit under the horse's jaw, and back on to the other side. There was a metal bar one foot in length with a medium strap. The man would then hold the horse away from him by means of the bar. This was designed especially so that they could control the horses.

In the show ring they still use outfits for showing off the smaller pony and cob stallions. There has been an intermittent demand for these to be made, and a recent one was for a pony with a back pad one and a half inches wide over the back.

Trotting horses in races run like an ordinary horse but the pacer has been trained to move his two left legs together and the two right legs together. The ponies are raced round a track at trotting speed and they must not canter or gallop. Handicapping is achieved by a timed countdown.

In America this racing is quite popular and they have race tracks for it. In England it is found in the North, around Manchester, and in Wales. There are a number of meetings each year on temporary tracks fenced by ropes, rather like motorcycle grass-track meetings, complete with bookmakers as well. I have made up various parts of the harness peculiar to this form of racing, but it is really a specialist's job.

Trotting races are becoming increasingly popular.

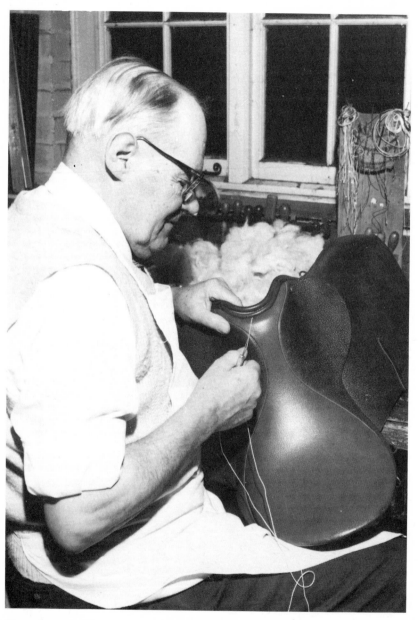

The author sews into place the front of the panel of a riding saddle.

7
Making a saddle

The word 'saddle' in saddler's jargon refers to any piece of equipment which fits over the horse's back to carry weight, such as a riding saddle, cart saddle or gig saddle.

Saddles are built in two parts: the outside part, which takes the wear of the leather backband or chain, and the inside, which fits the horse's back and is properly called the panel.

The cart saddle's panel was stuffed with straw with a layer of flock next to the horse and the riding saddle was stuffed with wool. The gig saddle, however, was stuffed with doe hair, and the facings were lined with brown paper which had been damped and rolled to shape with a board.

The only part of a saddle which was pigskin was the seat. The rest of it was made of cowhide, though there are saddles about now with suede inserts for gripping by the knees.

Saddles follow fashion like so many other things. In my early days no one wanted saddles with any pads or fittings on the flaps. The theory was that if one was thrown forward and got one's knees over the knee rolls it was difficult to get back into the saddle again. My father would not have dreamed of having any saddle unless the flap was absolutely straight.

Saddle design starts with the tree and the steel arch which fits over the horse's withers, for it is most important that the load should not rest on the animal's backbone. This could cause permanent injury. Horses vary a lot in size and shape of back but a tree known as a 'general fit' will suit many, although special fitting is often done.

To obtain a good fit we took a piece of striplead, for example lead piping hammered flat, and then carefully bent it to the shape of the horse's back. This was then put on a sheet of paper and drawn around. From that we would assess the type of tree required.

A horse with very narrow withers would need a saddle with a very high head and extra stuffing to clear the withers. That would be very unbalanced, so accordingly we cut back the head to allow the saddle to sit on each side of the withers.

At the end of the Second World War, when showjumping became popular in England, the Italians brought over a saddle called a 'Pariani' after the saddler who invented it. It had big knee rolls and thigh pads and was built on a 'spring tree'.

The modern jumping saddle is also built on a spring tree, which embodies strips of spring steel, producing a thin saddle with a flexible seat, and enables the rider to sit close to the horse's back. This type of tree had been made for years, but it was not until after the war that it came into prominence with the popularity of showjumping.

Saddles in the 1920s were nearly always lined in white serge. After the stuffing in the serge of the saddles had bedded down they would be returned to us for extra stuffing, known as back stuffing, and we used then to cover them with linen so that the horse's sweat could be washed off. The process produced a very accurately fitting saddle. Today leather-lined saddles are preferred.

In the 1920s a rider who was going to hounds might have to ride five or six miles to the meet, to be there by eleven in the morning. He would then be in the saddle until about three or four o'clock in the afternoon, with another five or six miles to ride back home. Unless a saddle was an absolutely perfect fit on the horse's back it would rub a sore in the same way that a badly fitted set of horseshoes would ruin the horse's feet. Today horses are taken in a horsebox to the meet, ridden for a couple of hours or so, and then put back in the horsebox and taken home.

The old riders, to a man, rode with fairly long stirrups in 'cavalry' or military style, while many riders today ride 'short'. This is all right, provided one rides with the weight in the middle or centre of the saddle.

After I had been at the trade ten years or so and had become a proficient saddler, I did a lot of work fitting and adjusting ladies' sidesaddles. Prior to the Second World War I was often called to fit and adjust these sidesaddles at the owners' premises. This was a job I was never keen to do, for the saddler was always blamed for any damage or mark on the horse's back, even if it had been caused by bad riding.

The riding saddle is made in two parts, as mentioned earlier. It is built on a 'tree' which is made of wood and reinforced with steel plates. The outer covering is grained cowhide and the actual seat pigskin. The panel is made from basil, which is sheepskin that has had the wool removed from the skin during the tanning process. The lining may be serge or leather. During construction the various parts are nailed to the tree with tacks of different lengths and thicknesses.

There is a new development in that some of the trees for the cheaper classes of saddle are now made of plastic and metal. A soft type of plastic is also used for panel work. These panels are not particularly satisfactory at present as they tend to split.

A typical gentleman's hunting saddle would be built on an eighteen

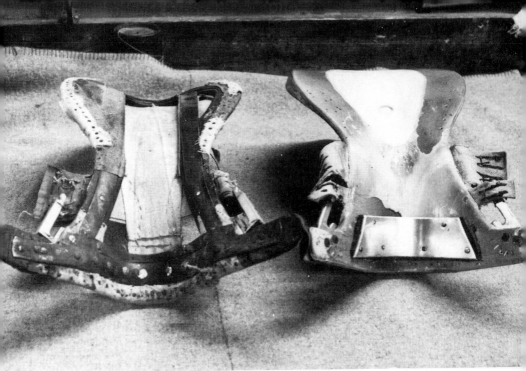

Riding saddle trees. The one on the right is plastic. That on the left is a spring tree, and the leather has been cut away to show the steel spring.

by eleven inch solid tree with a general purpose fitting. A lady's would be similar but on a seventeen by ten inch tree. When the wooden trees were nailed in the old days the nails rusted and accordingly they gripped very well.

There are a number of standard saddles built on general fitting trees; some have sloped heads and others may be plain, full cut back or half cut back. The head of a saddle is very strong and it is most important that it should stand clear of the animal's backbone or serious damage would be caused. A broken tree is usually caused by a fall. These saddles are all shaped to enable the withers of the horse to stand up through the front, and with the use of a thin layer of stuffing the rider sits close to the animal's back.

The half and full cut saddles are very useful to have as general purpose saddles in a stable where a number of saddles are needed to change round and to suit every kind of horse that comes in.

Some years ago I sold to a gentleman a saddle with a full cut-back head. He was master of a pack and was building up a collection of saddles. He came back to me and said he was not very happy with it. Later I tried to buy back the saddle in question, but he would not part with it as it had been discovered that what I had said earlier was true.

A sidesaddle with doeskin seat.

It fitted more horses than any other kind of saddle he had in stock, and he would not part with it for any price.

When building a special saddle the first job is to determine the length from the front to the back and the width of the seat. These depend on the height of the rider and the measurement from his hip to his knee, which decide where the knee will grip and where he will sit.

Webbing is fitted on the seat, and there are several operations involved in this. The webbing has been 'fired', which means that every bit of stretch in it has been taken out. It is fixed to the head, and the cantle and cross piece are nailed in place to make a firm base. The shape of the seat is built up from the side of the cantle by the belly pads, which are stuffed to give the shape and size of the seat. The seat is padded and covered with serge.

In high-quality saddles a small hole about one and a half inches long was cut in the centre of the seat serge and every bit of the stuffing was put in through the hole and worked into place with a long pointed seat awl. It was a very long process. Each little bit of wool was as big as the end of a thumb nail.

The pigskin for the seat proper would then be cut, soaked in water, stretched over the seat and temporarily tacked into place.

The skirts or side pieces of the saddle would then be put in position and marked. The skirts themselves would be thinned down, so that the two seams on each side of the seat might be joined on to them. A piece of 'piping' a quarter of an inch wide had then to be cut and thinned down to the thickness of paper. This had to be folded in half and tacked into place along the edge of the skirts.

When the seat was sewn into place the saddler picked up the stitch holes from the opposite side so that every stitch went straight through the centre of that small piece of piping. The piping was then an eighth of an inch wide. When stitching it into place it was most important that one did not stretch the seat or gather in any part of the leather which should not be gathered in.

Underneath the skirts straining pieces were fitted in order to strain the seat into position. The seat was then tacked underneath the tree.

The girth straps, three on each side, two of which were sewn and the third nailed on, were put into position and flaps were nailed on the tree. The D-shaped metal fittings to carry sandwich cases and any other hunting equipment were then put on. That finished the body or top of the saddle.

The lining was a separate section. The old style would be to cut it out of basil and parts would be lined to stiffen it up. It would be cut out exactly to shape, and across the front edge and round the seat edge it was stitched to the 'facings', pieces of pigskin an inch wide, sewn and then turned over to round the edge. The lining would be stitched in, inside out. Sometimes the saddler would whip it in by hand, and then it would be turned, with the panel the right way out. The facings were made by pushing white wool up in rolls and holding them by means of running or quilting stitches.

A full serge panel, which came to the bottom or three quarters of the way down the flaps, was quilted in order to stop the wool or stuffing slipping to the bottom. It was important to use the minimum quantity of wool in the quilted section to keep the panel thin. This was all done by hand.

The saddler would then stitch up the 'gullets', the part that runs directly under the horse's back and is so arranged that, with padding on each side of it, there is an air space under it so that it does not touch any bones.

Next the panel was stitched into place with a strong thread and half-moon needle. This was a very hard job. There were different types of lining, half-panel or a leather panel with felt known as a 'whippy' pattern.

The panel or stuffed part of a saddle is fitted into place. Note the pocket to take the point of the tree. In all types of saddle – cart, gig or riding – the panel is made as a separate part.

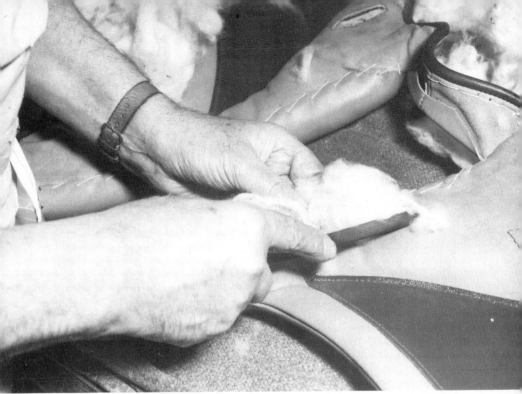

The author stuffs the panel of a saddle with wool. As little wool as possible had to be used in order to keep the panel thin.

The full serge saddle with linen is the best type, as it can be washed and the stuffing can be arranged better than in any other fashion — that is a saddler's reasoning.

When the panel is fitted into position using the seat awl, the final stuffing can be adjusted in the seat to the exact position, which is something that cannot be done on a leather saddle. The stuffing can be easily manoeuvred this way. When it comes back to be finally back-stuffed the stuffing is then put into position and held there with long stitches. The very thin quilting inside the leg grips the horse's flank and holds the saddle on to the horse.

The modern rider who looks after his horse and tack himself prefers the leather-lined saddle because it is easier to keep clean, but it should be remembered that the grooms of yesteryear were professionals in the care of horse and harness.

8
Types of leather

Leather first of all goes to the tannery, and there they clean it up and cut off the spare fat and bad bits. That done, it is cleaned in a lime pit, and then dehaired by friction.

The skin is then cleaned, washed and put into the various tan-pits. Years ago it was almost entirely done by oak-bark tannage. There are only one or two tanneries that use this method today. Usually they have much quicker methods and call it vegetable tannage. There is also a further method known as chrome tan.

In vegetable or oak-bark tannage, the hide is tanned until the liquor has passed right through the leather. The tanner periodically takes a bit out and makes a cut in the leather to see whether this has happened.

When it is soaked the leather is taken out, washed, dried and hung out. The tanner does many things with it, including treating it so that it does not turn black when exposed to the air.

The leather is finished by the currier. There are many processes used in the finishing. Some cowhides are split in two, producing an area of about one hundred square feet. The top half is known as 'split hide' and the bottom as 'hide split'.

The top one is used for high-grade work, casemaking for example. The bottom one has a mock finish put on it and is used for the cheaper grades of leatherwork such as school bags.

All the various grainings, finishes and colourings and stainings are then done by the currier to complete the work of the tanner.

Cowhide is the leather most used in saddlery. A hide is about fifty to fifty-five square feet in area, but for the saddler's use that hide would be split from head to tail to give two sides. It would then be split again from head to tail about two thirds of the distance from the centre of the back of the belly, producing a pair of 'backs' and a pair of 'bellies'. For saddlery work we used the backs.

There are never any two pieces of leather alike. They vary according to the place of origin, the type of animal, its breeding and its diet.

Leather which comes off a 'dead' animal – one which died, as against an animal which has been killed – is unsatisfactory. On one occasion I changed suppliers because I felt I was getting too many 'dead' skins. As the leather was folded, it cracked. If leather has been dressed and is workable it is all right, and I have had hides which cracked no matter what one did. Most suppliers would replace hides without question if referred back to them. They have replaced hides on my word alone, before now, without my sending a hide back.

The best parts of cowhide leather are used for the places which get the most wear, such as the traces and the reins. As they got lower down we would cut out a strapping which was not receiving so much use and yet taking the same amount of strain. The trace bears the whole weight of the vehicle, so this would be cut from the very best part of the back, whereas the loin strap, which is a carrier strap, supporting the breeching on the horse's back, could very well be of some leather not quite so good.

The saddler was always very choosy about his leather and took the best advantage of it down to the last scrap.

The next most common leather is pigskin with the hair removed. Pigskin as used for a saddle is not much more than two and a half or three millimetres thick. The pigskins are specially tanned for the job. For a wallet one would have a skin which had come off a very young animal, specially dressed and very thin.

Basil is bark-tanned sheepskin, being a corruption of 'basan' or 'bazan' from the French *basane*.

Buff leather was originally made from hide of the European buffalo, whence its name, but afterwards from horse or cattle hide. Its characteristic pale yellow colour, lightness and roughened surface arise from the oil dressing process known as shamoying.

Calf leather is in the strict sense from skins of unweaned animals and is thin and supple, with a close, fine grain.

In the eighteenth century leather was made from fish skin and frequently used for covering small articles. Little is known of its production, but it was apparently made from skins of plaice or other flat fish. It had a very fine granular surface and was usually stained black.

Cattle hides were normally vegetable tanned and had a natural thickness of four millimetres or more. When required thinner they were hand-shaved with a currier's knife. Early in the nineteenth century machines came into use which split the hide into several usable layers, of which only the top layer, having the 'grain' surface, was suitable for exterior work. This is 'split hide'. Raw or untanned hide is not really leather and is spoiled by wet or damp. When wet it is extremely plastic and can readily be moulded, for example into a quiver for archers' arrows.

Morocco leather is vegetable tanned goatskin, having a characteristic granular surface produced by 'boarding' it – that is by folding the leather, grain inwards, and rolling it back and forth with a cork-covered board in several directions. A simple kind of morocco was apparently introduced into Europe from North Africa, but it probably came originally from Babylonia, which was famous for its red goatskin.

Russian leather was originally a thin cattle hide made in Russia. It was tanned with willow and poplar bark, then treated with birch tar oil, giving it a peculiar odour. It was coloured red and brown and decorated with diced patterns. It was used mainly for upholstery and bookbinding in the eighteenth century.

Shagreen, as used from the seventeenth century, was not strictly leather. It was commonly made from untanned ray-fish skin, whose surface was covered with tiny globular protuberances. These were ground down until the surface was left smooth. Dye, usually green in colour, was then supplied to the flesh side, so that it seeped through between the circular formations, producing a beautiful pattern of colour.

Vellum was an opaque or translucent material with a carefully smoothed surface, usually made from calfskin, which was dehaired, degreased and dried out, untanned. It was used in ancient times mainly for writing and for bookbinding, but also for covering caskets. Parchment was made similarly from sheepskin.

Leather has the remarkable property that, when wet, it can be moulded into a shape, which it retains permanently if 'set' by the application of heat. The process was used in very early times for protective armour and throughout the middle ages for all kinds of bottles, flasks and boxes. Ornamentation was applied whilst the leather was still damp and remained sharply defined in the finished article. The term generally used in medieval times was *cuir bouilli,* but the reason is obscure, because no leather then made could be boiled. The method used today is essentially the same as in the past.

The principal methods of ornamenting the surface of leather are modelling (from the train or flesh side), punching (with metallic punches as in Spanish leather belts), incising, staining, painting (for example with tempera), inlaying and applying gold, silver and tin foils.

9
The saddler's diverse skills

Blacksmiths, carpenters, wheelwrights and shoemakers were all customers of the saddler and in many jobs their work overlapped. We often used to repair a set of bellows, for the house or for the blacksmith. I enjoyed recovering the carved and fancy-shaped antique bellows, but I used to hate repairing the blacksmith's bellows because I would finish up looking like a chimneysweep.

In the life of the village the horse was called upon for a variety of work. Some farms had a cider mill, which would be housed in one of the buildings together with all the equipment for cidermaking, for it was a winter job. The apples were placed in a circular stone trough and the horse was harnessed to a heavy stone wheel which he pulled round and round to crush the fruit thoroughly.

Sometimes one or more horses were harnessed to a revolving wheel known as a gin. Each horse was fastened to a spoke rather like a spoke of a capstan to provide the power to drive a set of shafting to which were attached a number of machines.

We made items for veterinary surgeons, including a particular prolapse harness for calving. We still make them occasionally. There were the spiked calf muzzles, used to wean calves, which were attached to the noses of the calves, so that the cows shied away when they approached.

We made dog boots to protect the feet of injured dogs and protective coverings like kneecaps, hockboots and tail guards to protect horses in transit. There were all types of boots for horses, for training, racing or hunting. There were many standard patterns but we were always prepared to vary them when required.

We used to make lawnboots regularly for horses pulling the lawnmowers and rollers on cricket pitches and playing fields. We also made poultice boots for horses.

At the Girls' High School, Hereford, a man named Teddy Mayo was hired with his horse to pull the mower. The groundsman, a rather stout gentleman, guided the machine whilst Teddy led the horse, but the trouble was that Teddy was paid a contract rate and the other man was paid a weekly wage. Accordingly the horse was kept moving at a very smart pace, somewhat to the discomfort of the groundsman.

We also made a variety of goods to order in waterproof canvas, including cases and covers for high-grade travel goods and musical instruments, rucksacks, gun covers and bags for specific requirements. Such items as presentation cases, blotters, hand-sewn pigskin cartridge bags and belts we took in our stride, and we still make card cases, comb cases and perhaps a case for four to five cigarettes. One man had a case to put a bottle of hair oil in; another had to have a box of Swan Vestas matches covered.

One customer came in and I happened to have a piece of reptile skin in stock, purely by accident. I thought he would like it and showed it to him. I made a wallet from it, and there is not another like it in the country. It was in a particular style and from an unusual skin. We cannot cope with all the items we could make and sell.

I have made cases for photographic equipment and for one press photographer with an expensive camera and a range of fittings I designed and made a case which enabled him to remove any item without disturbing the rest. It took quite some time to work out but that is one of the joys of being a craftsman.

I have made and taught handbag making, also hand-tooled leatherwork, but I would not attempt to compete with a handbag manufacturer.

One of the first things I ever made was a case to carry a dummy upright piano for a firm of piano factors as they wanted to show off this highly French-polished piano to people.

We repaired all kinds of travel goods, putting in new locks and zips. We had to be pretty skilful locksmiths, fitting new keys, adjusting locks and repairing them.

These days there are not many trunks to be repaired. People used to buy tickets in advance, and sent their trunks on, before they went on holiday. School trunks are still in demand but as nowadays parents very often take their children and trunks by road to and from school there is very little repair work needed.

The largest member of the trunk family was the imperial trunk, which was built on a basket frame with a soft lining of cotton. Outside was thick canvas, blackened over, with a shiny surface, and the edges of the trunk were bound with leather. It was so big that a man could not reach inside to stitch a patch on the bottom. The saddler would be outside the trunk, pushing the awl through it, and the boy would be inside the trunk, returning the needle through the hole. The apprentice was never very excited about this arrangement.

I have repaired and repainted several old-fashioned rocking horses. They each had to be fitted with a new saddle, bridle and reins and it gave me great enjoyment as they were so well made.

On one occasion the Bishop of Hereford sent his car to the shop at nine o'clock in the morning and it was collected at six o'clock the

A saddler's workshop, with the author (left) and his colleagues at work.

same evening. In that time a completely new green baize interior had been fitted into the car.

The old horse fairs brought more people into the town and that meant the sale of halters for the horses, red, white and blue ribbons and rosettes and items for plaiting the horses' manes – a yard and a half of each of these colours was just sufficient.

In the summer we even used to sell earcaps to keep the flies out of horses' ears, and one or two tradespeople bought straw hats for the horses to wear.

The saddler was also expected to be an expert at splicing ropes, putting on whippings and similar jobs. He also repaired whips, putting on 'keepers' and binding and covering them with leather. I sometimes fitted or repaired lift ropes, too.

To protect the men's hands and arms from thorns when they were laying hedges, they wore very heavy leather mittens known as hedging gloves. The leather used was either chrome-dressed cowhide or sealskin and the pieces were sewn together with a white thong made from horsehide.

In the 1920s a man came to us who had been trained to make hedging gloves on a bigger scale. We soon developed this into a big business, producing in the region of three thousand pairs a year. It took an hour to make a pair, so during the Slump we had three thousand hours of guaranteed work, a great boon to a small shop.

At that time I had two top-grade saddlers with me, and we three could make twenty-four pairs of hedging gloves each day. At one period, when pushed and pressed for them, I have made fourteen pairs a day myself. Two of us made fourteen pairs each per day in fact, and we worked all day, making eight pairs at work, and then took six pairs home to make up working until one o'clock in the morning. I got a shilling a pair for them, making fourteen shillings for fourteen hours very hard but welcome work.

It shows how hard craftsmen and tradesmen used to work in those days because since the war I have never had any man working for me who could make more than three pairs of gloves in a day. There is not the drive to do it, or the skill and speed.

Demand since has fluctuated but with hedge trimmers of all kinds and sizes now available there is nothing like the old demand for the gloves.

From time to time we made head collars, leather halters and other items for Hereford cattle. I first made them in the 1920s to go to Argentina, to a Captain Hinks, who was a Hereford breeder. He had to have stamped across the collars the words *El Cabana, Capitan Hinks*. After the war there was an upsurge in the breeding and export of Hereford cattle and we began to make large numbers of collars.

Nowadays we make three types, each in three sizes. The Export is a plain training collar. The others are much more elaborate and are meant for showing off the animal in the ring and as presentation collars and they have brass fittings and brass rings.

About that period I knew the late Captain de Quincey, the famous breeder of the Herefordshire Vern Herd. For him a special collar was designed which I called the Vern or de Quincey head collar. These we make and send out worldwide.

To be correct, the horns of the Hereford bull have to be bent forward and downwards, and since they do not always grow like this several things are done to encourage them to do so, such as attaching lead cups, cast to fit the ends of the horns, in three different weights, which are strapped on and left to weigh the horns down. Occasionally we make a single leather cup to use on one horn, a lead weight being

OPPOSITE: *A Hereford bull wears a head collar made by the author's firm. The collar is made in brown work and so there is no final varnishing as there would be on black harness work.*

The Davis Horn Trainer, designed by the author to encourage the bull's horns to grow to the approved shape.

used on the other horn. Once in a while the herdsmen make a heavyweight one to pull them down at the last minute.

I designed the 'Davis Horn Trainer', which had leather cups and rubber springs. It had a fulcrum or turning effect with a weight on the nose to bring the horns forwards and downwards. These horn trainers have been sent to many parts of the world, and we have had repeat orders by the score.

One of my presentation collars was sent to the King of Sweden, in 1977, when he was presented with a Hereford bull. Reports tell that he was more interested in the special collar than in the bull itself.

The leather head collar, plain or fancy, was designed particularly for leading the bull in the ring. It was not intended to be strong enough to tie him up, so herdsmen use a neck strap, a very strong one, some four feet six inches long by two inches wide, with a very heavy buckle and a metal D. It goes round the neck of the animal and the rope is fixed to the D. Most breeders use this when they come out of the ring. The collars then come off the animals.

10
The saddler's tools

In Hereford Museum today is a display of saddlers' tools, part of which I presented.

I had a mark on my tools which was intended to distinguish mine from those of other saddlers and most workmen would either put their name or have a special mark on their tools. There were items which were always provided by the master saddler but the ordinary run of the mill tools were the workmen's own. My mark was a St Andrew's cross joined across the top, which I filed on the handle of the tool.

The round knife was the saddler's most handy tool, used for cutting out and shaping leather, and it was in his hand pretty well all the time.

There were tools known as edge-shaves, which were used to take the sharp edge off the leather after it had been cut. They were in varying widths, each with a channel to make a cut of a particular width.

The saddler used a plough gauge to cut his straps. Normally we took a large side of leather six feet six inches long, made a straight edge along the best side and cut straight strips from that edge.

The saddler's tools.

A close-up of the pricking iron shown in use on page 28. Note the angle of the prongs.

Finishing tools were used to burnish the edges of leather and for creasing the edges by putting a little narrow line around the edge.

A burnisher was normally the tool of a groom and was made of chain links on a leather backing. It was used for cleaning and polishing the bits, in the days when these were all made of steel. It was about three inches by three inches, being a natural hand size. A fiddle burnisher was the shape of a violin bow, only much shorter and wider, about four links wide, and it would rub across the steel to produce a shine.

The military sometimes used a narrow sack partly filled with sand and pieces of torn-up brown paper. One end of the sack was tied off and fitted to a hook. The articles to be burnished were then put inside this sack, which was pulled to and fro sending the items backwards and forwards through the sand and paper mixture.

Another tool in the museum is a pair of blocks and a press for making carthorse winkers. The leather was cut out and soaked until very soft and then put between the blocks and a pressure of about half a ton was applied. They were then left to dry out.

11
Changing times

During the slump of the 1930s many saddlers went under as the use of draught horses declined. My employer had been sufficiently far-seeing to extend his range to include sports goods and this became an important aspect of the business, for it coincided with the closure of two local shops and for a time we had a local monopoly.

However, saddlery now is in greater demand for riding than when I started work and of course we have incorporated fancy goods too, and in later years we went into the production and selling of many types of goods.

During that period I learned to do many different types of work on sports equipment, such as stringing all types of tennis and badminton rackets and recovering billiard tables.

I was always interested in craftwork and took lessons, which I found assisted me in the performance of my trade. When I was about forty I took up part-time teaching and was able to run successful classes in leatherwork and handicrafts of various kinds. As I was in-

The prolapse harness is an example of the veterinary work undertaken by the saddler.

vited to attend other craft lessons run by the Education Department I gained many an insight into other crafts.

When the cathedral close was opened up and our shop was pulled down my employer purchased a shop in Commercial Street, our present premises. What a boon this enforced move turned out to be, for at the time our shop staff was Mr Ellis, three saddlers, an office girl and an errand boy. A new workshop was built on what had been the garden and I became shop foreman; not always an easy job, for some of the men were old enough to be my father.

After the Second World War we settled down and we now had in the workshop four saddlers, a woman hand stitcher and a machinist. However as the old hands retired there were no replacements, and we have come down to two, each working for only a few hours per week.

Today my expertise could be used over and over again, because of the revival of driving for pleasure and riding, but sad to say, yet understandably so, not many young people are coming into the trade as I did, those many years ago.

Index